Totally White

& other poems
of life & love

VC Press
Pleasant Grove, UT

VC Press
an imprint of
Rosehaven Publishing Group
P.O. Box 247
Pleasant Grove, UT 84062

ISBN
978-1-931858-23-6

Design & Typesetting
LibrisPro.com

Cover Illustration
istockphoto.com
"Valentine Gift Tag" by hatman12

Internal Illustrations
clipart.com
p. 16 © 2007 Kristi Miles; used with permission.

For my mother,
Lucille Wells,
who encouraged me to write
& set an example for me to follow

Totally White

& Other Poems of Life & Love

The poems in the Totally White collection
were written from 1979 to 1980 as a
thematic collection for an advanced
creative writing project.

Having been stricken
by a case of hardened categories
he reached up into a 65 year old
box of black and white and,
lifting out a coon
which promptly bit him,
died.

Totally White

Being totally white
and of God's chosen race,
Katherine (Kate) Kooley
has trouble eating Oreo cookies
because they remind her of the time
Great Aunt Martha
(also totally white and of God's chosen race)
said the 'N' word
to Kate's boyfriend's face
and then pretended
not to notice when the poor man
tried to prove he was as good
as Uncle George
(also totally white and of God's chosen race)
in chess.

He took the white pieces,
of course,
but couldn't quite
bring himself to checkmate
his soul.

Under the Golden Arches

When I finally fell in love
my friends and I
went out to celebrate
with Big Macs and Hot Apple Pies.
They were happy
and full of questions.
So of course
I told them you were kind,
and gentle,
and most of all,
you loved me.

Then I told them your face
    was creamy smooth,
like a milk shake.
My friends laughingly asked,
"what flavor?"

When I said, "chocolate"
they dropped their french fries
and left.

Chocolate Kisses

He blew them chocolate kisses
to prove he is in love
but I shielded with supremacy
all over And above
the bright sun shined all hot
and melt them into gross
and my Willy Wonka factory
got lost to me—
almost.

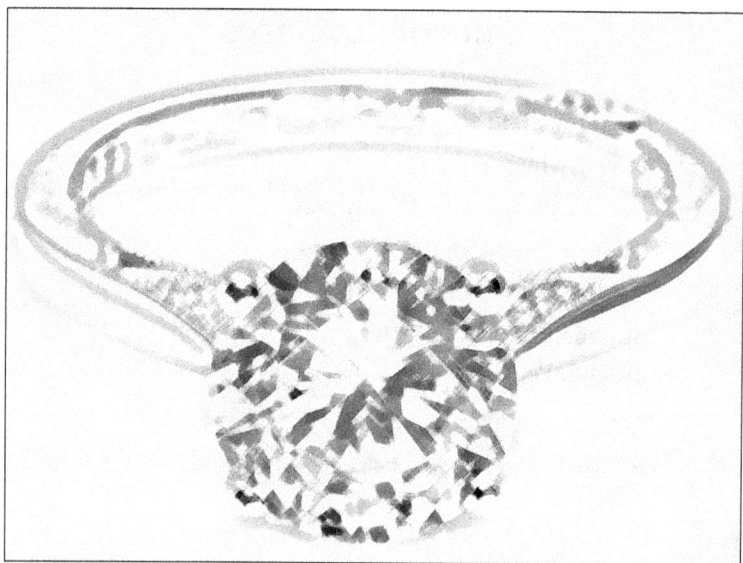

Dear Dad

We went to buy a bunny
when I was only three
and when it came to picking one
the choice was up to me.
When I chose the pink one
even though you liked the blue,
you hugged me tight and kissed my cheek
and said, "I still love you."

Then when I went to buy a dress
for my first high school dance,
you came along to help me find
a dress made for romance.
And when I chose the white one
even though you liked the pink,
you smiled and squeezed my fingers warm
and said, "Do what you think."

And when I searched for one to love
the choice again was mine
and all you said was, "Just be sure
you find someone who's kind."

Today I choose the brown one,
even though you like the white.
I hope that you will love me still
and say that it's alright.

Milk-Brown Babies

They really don't seem to care:
that you can give me
a warm home
with two cars in the garage
and a cat by the fireplace;

that you hold my hand real tight
when you say you love me;

that you smile
when I laugh
and cry
when I frown;

that we love each other more than
color
upward mobility
and social stratification.

All they can see with their white eyes
is that you'll give me milk-brown babies.

The Coon Commandments

"Never fight a white man,
never turn your head,
and never, ever any night
take a white girl to bed."

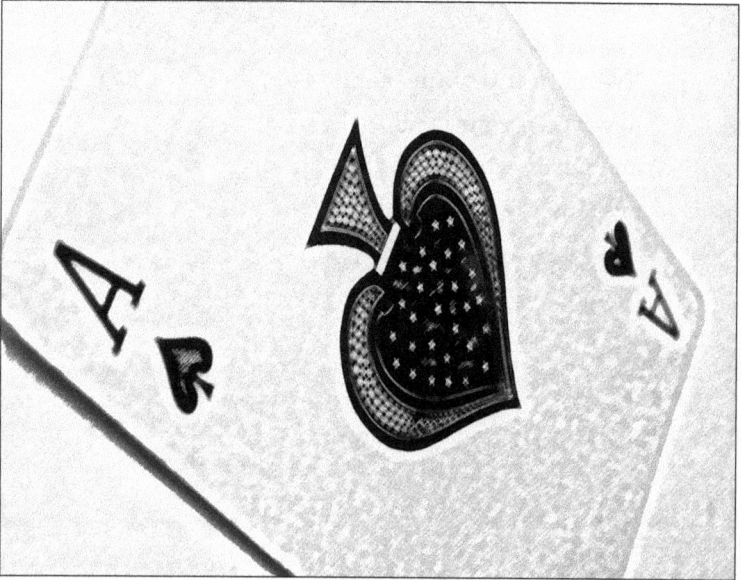

Ace of Spades

(Monday nights
we stay home
and play cards
and I always thought
she let me win
until one night
of High Card Draw,
after fighting
over points and bets,
she suddenly kissed me
and laughed,
    "But I always win
    because I hold the Ace of Spades.")

"...so much depends
upon

the milk chocolate
baby,

diapered and
pinned,

in the arms of
the creamy white
woman..."

*In the style of "The Red Wheelbarrow"
by William Carlos Williams

Other Poems of Life & Love

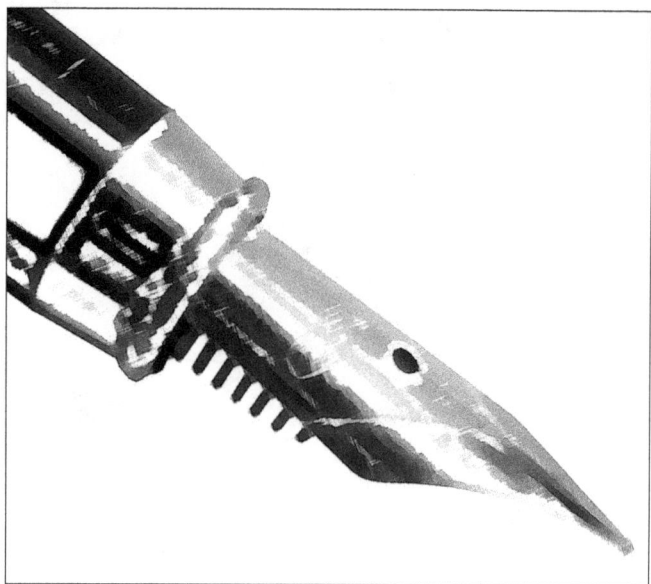

Writing

white paper
stained with marks of blue and red
drops of sadness,
drops of anger,
mingled with the drops of love.

today I want
tomorrow I need
yesterday was just a dream
cloudy movements
drift softly by
on their way to bloom
cyclone of fury
washed up on the beach
surf foam
drying in the yards
with backdoor laundry
hanging out to air
dogs bark
to running flesh and fur
and mice
complete the end of the game

life's a mystery
but it flows from a pen
to find
white paper
stained with marks of blue and red
drops of sadness,
drops of anger,
mingled in with drops of love.

(1977)

Card Trick

We passed endless days
not knowing
not needing
each other's existence,
until the hands of fate
reshuffled our lives
and put us together
in a deck of unknowns.
we work
we play
we laugh and cry.
we learn
we grow
we live and die.
Together,
until a Joker
slips between us.

(1977)

Friends

You said
my life was like a jigsaw
with one of the pieces gone.

So you gave me one of yours
and I took it
because you were so kind
and I knew that you cared.

You didn't see me trim the edges
so it would match the gap
that I had made for it to fit in.

(1979)

I don't understand you
but I love you
I think
at least, I'd like to
But you won't let me
sometimes
and when you do
I'm never really sure
if you're with me,
or somewhere else
wishing you were here.

(1979)

27

Crying in the Room Next Door

They are crying in the room next door,
I can hear them through these paper thin walls.
He says that fall comes quickly,
and she promises to write.

You too are leaving
and we have no such promises,
you spoke no such words to me.

I roll over in bed,
squeeze my eyes shut,
and concentrate on the blackness,
while they cry in the room next door.

(1980)

Divergence

We cannot always
be together
but we won't always
be alone.
Our paths were one once
but now they've turned
different ways.

My feet can only be at peace
strolling my own path,
and you must find beauty
on yours,
for the separateness
and the division of our lives
shall serve to make us love each other more
when we meet again.

(1978)

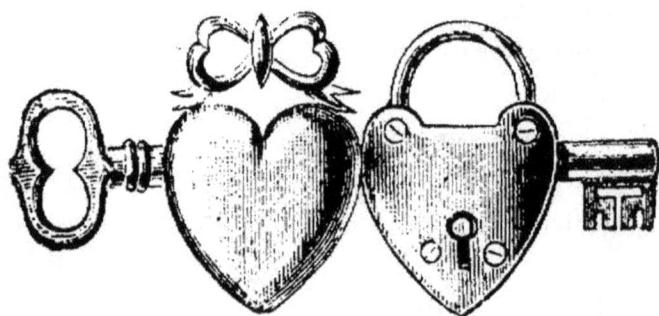

Tomorrow

When I write the song
I found in the snow and rain—
and it will be a sad song,
born of cold and pain—
Will you take it in your hands
and warm it until the chill has gone
and it has become a thing
that people can love?

(1979)

#218R

'Tis truth I find your mind appealing,
and I'm enchanted by the words you say.
Sent from the heart to the bright of day
they're polished with precision and feeling.

'Tis truth to see, your hair blows shining free
and in your deep brown eyes
    sweet laughter peals.
While dancing on your lips, a smile reveals
myriad esoteric thoughts to me.

'Tis truth these things have great attraction
and there are so many more could
    take their place—
your soft touch, gentle kiss, and warm embrace.
But they were not my first distraction.

All of these things my honesty refutes.
Twas your Calvin Klein jeans and navy boots.

(1979)

35

Spring

Beginnings are
breakable, tender things—
fragile
filigreed friendships,
heartfelt handfuls
of hope.
Needing, and knowing
it may not work,
Tenderly
trying anyway;
innumerable conflicts
constantly cascading
down to the
depths of laughter
life
and love.

(1978)

Who Are You?

Who are you?
Looking sideways
out of the corner of your eye,
hoping
I don't see you watching me.

Who are you?
Sneaking glances
starting smiles and
wondering
if I'm doing the same.

Who are you?
Did I know you
in another reach of time?
Were you
dear to my heart then
or just another stranger
passing by?

(1978)

Like pigeons in the attic
our love waits
for one of us to feed it
or set it free.

(1979)

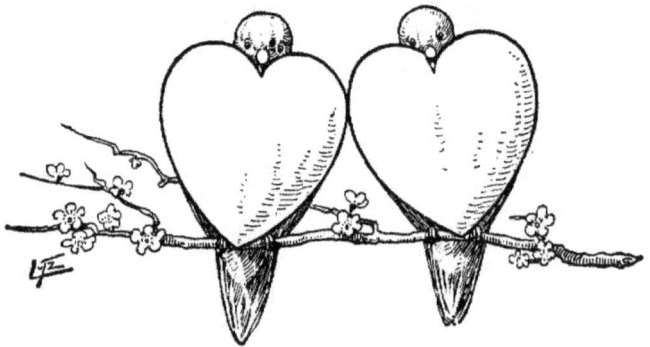

Special

I am no more special
than this man sitting next to me
with the bushy brown beard
which tickles the air when he moves.

Nor am I any different
than the old woman across the aisle,
dripping wrinkles from her face
and age spotted hands.

Nor do I have more to offer
than the young child up ahead
who may one day use his mind and heart
to help others.

But I have something
none of them have.
I have you—
your love
your confidence
your trust
your friendship.

These things make me unique in all the world.

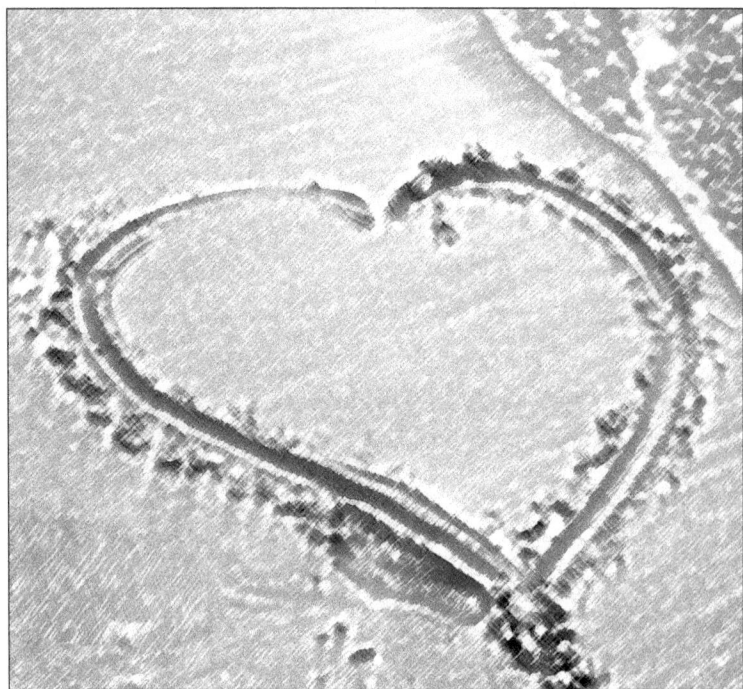

Eternity

One day
I wrote our names together in the sand
and drew a big heart
around them.
And then I sat and watched
as the tide came in
and washed it all away.

How sad,
my sister said,
as the waves carried the last traces of us
out into the horizon.

Perhaps.
But now you and I
are a part of the ocean
forever.

(1979)

The Gardner and His Rose

Once upon a midnight sky
I wished upon a star to die.
I whispered, "God, please let me go,"
Deep inside, He answered, "No."

Then He continued, this He said:
Never wish that you were dead.
You've many years left to live,
And I've many lessons yet to give.

Let your symbol be the rose.
Watch her as she tries to grow.
Though thorns may mar the beauty there,
The Gardener loves the clothes she wears.

She struggles through the wind and rain,
Her days of winter are a strain.
And though she sometimes bends and breaks
the Gardener mends these small mistakes.

And when she thinks her life in vain,
Or, by chance, encounters pain,

Or happily retires for bed,
The Gardener watches overhead.

And when her flowers are in full bloom,
the Gardener decorates his room.
And though her petals have wasted away
She is with the Gardener today.

And so my child, forget your fears
And if you will, live with your tears.
Rest easy and take good cheer,
for you know I am the Gardener here.

(1977)

Life stalks us as prey
and time after time
our souls are left bleeding,
hope slipping away.

Life stalks as we pray
but time after time
our souls fill with comfort
and strength for the day.

(1983)

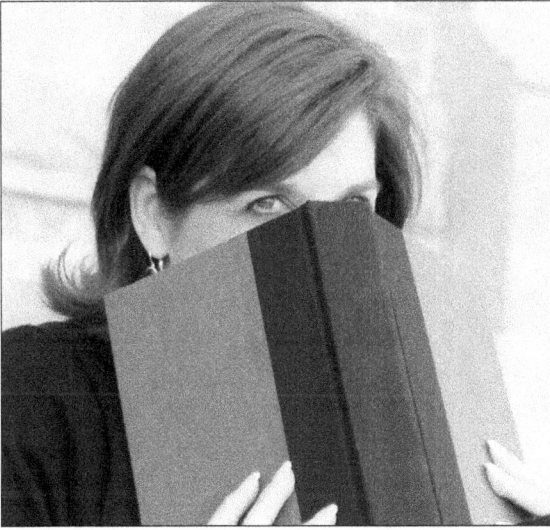

Karlene Wells has always loved making up poems and stories. When she went to college, she majored in exaggeration and hyperbole. This penchant for creative embellishment sometimes gets her into trouble. On occasion it provides entertainment to those around her. Either way, it's become a habit she cannot break.

Karlene lives in a happy little valley surrounded by very large mountains. When she's not at her computer writing, she enjoys spending time with her husband, children, and grandchildren.

www.ingramcontent.com/pod-product-compliance
Lightning Source LLC
Chambersburg PA
CBHW071735020426
42331CB00008B/2043